Psychosocial Problems Among Differently-Abled Elderly Persons

OrangeBooks Publication

1st Floor, Rajhans Arcade, Mall Road, Kohka, Bhilai, Chhattisgarh 490020

Website: **www.orangebooks.in**

© **Copyright, 2025, Author**

All rights reserved. No part of this book may be reproduced, stored in a retrieval system, or transmitted, in any form by any means, electronic, mechanical, magnetic, optical, chemical, manual, photocopying, recording or otherwise, without the prior written consent of its writer.

First Edition, 2025

ISBN: 978-93-6554-035-2

PSYCHOSOCIAL PROBLEMS
AMONG DIFFERENTLY-ABLED ELDERLY PERSONS

DR. DANISH SIDDIQUI

OrangeBooks Publication
www.orangebooks.in

Contents

Chapter 1
Introduction 1

Chapter 2
Problems & Challenges 4

Chapter 3
Continent-Wise Study 18

Chapter 4
Issues And Government Policies 34

Chapter 5
A Fictional Case Study 48

Chapter 6
Conclusion 57

Chapter 1
Introduction

Introduction

The psycho-social challenges faced by differently-abled individuals present a complex landscape where the interplay of psychological and social factors significantly influences their well-being and overall quality of life. Differently-abled persons, encompassing a diverse range of abilities and disabilities, often encounter a host of unique issues that extend beyond the physical aspects of their conditions. Understanding and addressing these psycho-social problems is pivotal for fostering inclusivity, dismantling societal barriers, and enhancing the holistic support structures necessary for the empowerment of individuals living with disabilities.

Diversity In Disability

Differently-abled individuals exhibit a rich tapestry of abilities and challenges, ranging from physical impairments to cognitive and sensory disabilities. This diversity underscores the need for personalized approaches that recognize the unique nature of each person's experience and the various ways in which disability can intersect with their identity.

Psychological Dimensions

Living with a disability can profoundly impact an individual's psychological well-being. Questions of self-identity, self-esteem, and coping mechanisms come to the forefront as individuals navigate societal perceptions and expectations. The emotional journey involves grappling with acceptance, resilience, and the construction of a positive self-image in the face of challenges.

Social Dynamics And Stigmatization

One of the significant psycho-social problems faced by differently-abled persons is the potential for social isolation and stigmatization. Prejudice, misconceptions, and a lack of awareness can lead to exclusionary behaviors, hindering social integration and contributing to feelings of alienation.

Educational And Employment Challenges

Obtaining access to quality education and equitable employment opportunities can be an uphill battle for differently-abled individuals. Systemic barriers, including a lack of accommodations and understanding, often limit their potential for educational and professional advancement, perpetuating socio-economic disparities.

Accessibility Barriers

Physical and environmental barriers pose significant challenges to differently-abled individuals. Inaccessible public spaces, transportation, and infrastructures can impede mobility, limit independence, and create hurdles to active participation in various aspects of life.

Caregiver Dynamics

The psycho-social landscape extends to the caregivers and families of differently-abled individuals. The emotional toll of caregiving, coupled with societal attitudes and the lack of adequate support structures, can contribute to caregiver stress and burnout.

Advocacy And Empowerment

Addressing psycho-social problems among differently-abled individuals necessitates robust advocacy efforts. Initiatives that challenge stereotypes, raise awareness about the diverse abilities of differently-abled persons, and promote inclusivity contribute to societal change. Empowering individuals with disabilities involves creating an environment where they can actively participate in and contribute to society.

In summary, the psycho-social problems faced by differently-abled individuals underscore the importance of cultivating a compassionate and inclusive society. By recognizing and addressing the unique challenges at the intersection of psychology and social dynamics, we move towards a more equitable and supportive environment that values the diverse contributions of all individuals, regardless of their abilities.

Chapter 2
Problems & Challenges

Psycho-Social Problems

Psycho-social problems encompass a broad range of challenges that affect an individual's mental and social well-being. These issues often arise from the interplay between psychological factors and the surrounding social environment. Some common psycho-social problems include:

- **Mental Health Disorders:** Conditions such as anxiety, depression, and mood disorders can significantly impact an individual's psychological well-being, influencing their ability to cope with everyday challenges.

- **Social Isolation:** Feelings of loneliness and a lack of social connections can lead to social isolation, which, in turn, can contribute to mental health issues and a diminished sense of belonging.

- **Stigma and Discrimination:** Individuals facing prejudice or discrimination based on factors like race, gender, sexual orientation, or disabilities may experience psycho-social problems, leading to stress, low self-esteem, and a sense of injustice.

- **Financial Stress:** Economic hardships and financial instability can contribute to mental health challenges, as individuals may grapple with anxiety, fear, and a reduced capacity to access essential resources and opportunities.

- **Relationship Strain:** Difficulties in interpersonal relationships, whether within families, friendships, or romantic partnerships, can result in psycho-social issues, impacting emotional well-being and overall life satisfaction.

- **Trauma and Post-Traumatic Stress:** Exposure to traumatic events can lead to post-traumatic stress disorder (PTSD) and other psycho-social difficulties, affecting an individual's ability to function and maintain healthy relationships.

- **Cultural and Societal Expectations:** The pressure to conform to societal norms and cultural expectations can contribute to stress and anxiety, particularly when individuals feel they do not meet these standards or face discrimination for deviating from them.

Addressing psycho-social problems often requires a holistic approach, integrating mental health services, social support networks, and efforts to reduce stigma and discrimination. Promoting understanding, empathy, and inclusivity within communities is crucial for creating environments that foster positive mental and social well-being.

Impact On Human Being

Psycho-social problems can have a profound impact on individuals, affecting various aspects of their lives and well-being. The consequences of these issues may manifest in physical, emotional, and social dimensions, leading to a range of challenges for the affected person. Here are some impacts of psycho-social problems on individuals:

1. **Mental Health Issues:** Psycho-social problems often contribute to or exacerbate mental health disorders such as anxiety, depression, and post-traumatic stress disorder (PTSD). The emotional toll can be overwhelming, affecting an individual's ability to think clearly, concentrate, and make sound decisions.

2. **Physical Health:** The stress associated with psycho-social problems can have adverse effects on physical health. It may lead to conditions such as insomnia, headaches, digestive problems, and a weakened immune system, making individuals more susceptible to illnesses.

3. **Impaired Social Functioning:** Social withdrawal and isolation are common consequences of psycho-social problems. Individuals may find it challenging to engage in social activities, maintain relationships, or communicate effectively, leading to feelings of loneliness and alienation.

4. **Reduced Quality of Life:** Psycho-social issues can diminish overall life satisfaction and hinder individuals from pursuing and enjoying life's opportunities. This reduction in quality of life may be evident in various areas, including work, education, and personal relationships.

5. **Impaired Coping Mechanisms:** Individuals facing psycho-social problems may struggle to cope with stressors and challenges effectively. Maladaptive coping mechanisms such as substance abuse, self-harm, or unhealthy behaviors may emerge as individuals attempt to manage their emotional distress.

6. **Impact on Relationships:** Psycho-social issues can strain relationships with family, friends, and colleagues. Difficulty in communicating emotions, social withdrawal, or mood swings may lead to misunderstandings and conflicts, further isolating the individual.

7. **Reduced Productivity and Functioning:** In work and academic settings, psycho-social problems can impair concentration, productivity, and performance. This can lead to absenteeism, decreased job satisfaction, and academic underachievement.

8. **Financial Consequences:** Some psycho-social problems, such as addiction or mental health disorders, may contribute to financial strain. Individuals may struggle with maintaining employment, budgeting, and overall financial stability.

Addressing psycho-social problems requires a comprehensive approach that may include counseling, therapy, social support, and interventions to improve overall well-being. Creating awareness, reducing stigma, and fostering supportive communities are essential steps in mitigating the impact of psycho-social problems on individuals.

Differently-Abled Persons

"Differently-abled persons" is a term used to describe individuals with disabilities or impairments. This more inclusive phrase emphasizes the unique abilities and potential of individuals, regardless of their physical, sensory, intellectual, or developmental differences. Here are some key points to consider when discussing differently-abled persons:

1. **Diverse Abilities:** People with disabilities have a wide range of abilities and talents. Using the term "differently-abled" recognizes that individuals may excel in various areas, even if they face challenges in certain aspects of life.

2. **Respect and Inclusion:** The term promotes a more respectful and inclusive language compared to outdated terms that may have negative connotations. It focuses on the person's capabilities rather than framing them solely in terms of their limitations.

3. **Empowerment:** Emphasizing "differently-abled" contributes to the empowerment of individuals with disabilities. It encourages a positive mindset and challenges societal stereotypes, fostering an environment where everyone is valued for their unique contributions.

4. **Person-First Language:** Person-first language is integral to discussions about differently-abled persons. This means acknowledging the person before the disability, reinforcing the idea that individuals are not defined solely by their impairments.

5. **Accessibility and Inclusion:** Differently-abled persons often face barriers related to accessibility and inclusion. Addressing these issues is crucial to ensure that everyone can participate fully in society, regardless of their abilities or disabilities.

6. **Advocacy for Rights:** The term aligns with the broader advocacy for the rights of individuals with disabilities. It emphasizes the need for equal opportunities, non-discrimination, and the creation of an accessible and inclusive environment for everyone.

7. **Education and Awareness:** Using inclusive language helps promote education and awareness about the diverse needs and experiences of differently-abled individuals. It encourages society to recognize and appreciate the strengths and potential of all its members.

It's important to note that preferences for terminology may vary among individuals, and some may prefer specific language based on their personal experiences and perspectives. Open communication and a willingness to learn about and respect individual preferences contribute to creating an inclusive and supportive society for differently-abled persons.

Differently-abled persons face a range of challenges that can impact various aspects of their lives. These challenges are often a result of societal attitudes, physical barriers, and the lack of inclusive policies. Some common problems faced by differently-abled persons include:

1. **Accessibility Barriers:** Physical environments, public spaces, and transportation systems are often not designed to accommodate individuals with disabilities. This lack of accessibility can restrict their mobility and independence.

2. **Social Stigma and Discrimination:** Differently-abled persons may encounter social stigma and discrimination, leading to exclusion from social activities, education, and employment opportunities. Negative stereotypes and misconceptions about disabilities contribute to these challenges.

3. **Limited Employment Opportunities:** Many differently-abled individuals face barriers in accessing employment opportunities. Employers may be hesitant to hire individuals with disabilities due to misconceptions about their abilities or concerns about accommodation costs.

4. **Inadequate Educational Support:** Access to quality education can be a significant challenge for differently-abled persons. Educational institutions may lack the necessary accommodations, resources, or trained staff to support the diverse needs of students with disabilities.

5. **Healthcare Disparities:** Differently-abled individuals may encounter disparities in healthcare, including challenges in accessing appropriate medical care, rehabilitation services, and assistive devices. This can affect their overall health and well-being.

6. **Financial Strain:** Managing the costs associated with disabilities, such as medical expenses, assistive devices, and accessible housing modifications, can pose a financial burden on differently-abled individuals and their families.

7. **Psychological Impact:** Coping with societal expectations, discrimination, and the daily challenges of living with a disability can lead to psychological stress and mental health issues. Support for mental well-being is crucial for individuals facing these challenges.

8. **Lack Of Inclusive Policies:** In many regions, there is a lack of comprehensive and inclusive policies that address the needs of differently-abled persons. This includes inadequate legal protections, accessibility standards, and social welfare programs.

9. **Transportation Challenges:** Accessible and reliable transportation is often a significant issue for differently-abled persons. Public transportation may not be wheelchair accessible, and private transportation options can be limited and expensive.

10. **Communication Barriers:** Differently-abled individuals who experience communication disabilities may face challenges in expressing themselves and accessing information. The lack of inclusive communication tools and technologies can contribute to social isolation.

Addressing these problems requires a concerted effort from society, policymakers, and communities to promote inclusivity, eliminate discrimination, and create environments that accommodate the diverse needs and abilities of differently-abled individuals. Implementing and enforcing inclusive policies and fostering awareness are key steps toward building a more accessible and supportive society.

Elderly Persons

"Elderly persons" refers to individuals who are in the later stages of their life, typically considered senior citizens or seniors. This term is used to describe people in the later decades of their lifespan, generally 65 years and older. Here are some key considerations when discussing elderly persons:

1. **Diversity:** The term "elderly persons" encompasses a diverse group with a wide range of experiences, backgrounds, and health statuses. It's essential to recognize the individuality of each person within this demographic.

2. **Respect And Dignity:** Using the term "elderly persons" emphasizes the importance of treating older individuals with respect and dignity. It acknowledges the wisdom, experience, and contributions that come with age.

3. **Aging Population:** Many societies around the world are experiencing an aging population as life expectancy increases. This demographic shift has implications for healthcare, social services, and the overall structure of communities.

4. **Health And Well-Being:** The health and well-being of elderly persons are significant considerations. Providing access to healthcare, addressing age-related health issues, and promoting healthy aging are crucial components of supporting this demographic.

5. **Social Inclusion:** Social isolation and loneliness can be challenges for elderly persons. Encouraging social inclusion, community engagement, and intergenerational activities are important for maintaining a sense of connection and well-being.

6. **Care and Support:** As individuals age, there may be a need for additional care and support. This could include family assistance, community services, or residential care facilities. Ensuring accessible and compassionate care for elderly persons is a societal responsibility.

7. **Active Aging:** Many older individuals lead active and fulfilling lives. The concept of "active aging" encourages seniors to remain engaged in social, cultural, and recreational activities, promoting overall health and well-being.
8. **Elder Abuse Prevention:** Protecting elderly persons from abuse, neglect, and exploitation is a critical concern. Raising awareness and implementing measures to prevent elder abuse contribute to the safety and security of older individuals.
9. **Policy Considerations:** Policymakers often address the needs of the elderly population through social policies, healthcare initiatives, and retirement support programs. Creating age-friendly communities and considering the specific needs of elderly persons in policy decisions is important.

Understanding the diverse needs and experiences of elderly persons is essential for creating age-inclusive and supportive communities. It involves recognizing and valuing the contributions of older individuals while addressing the challenges associated with aging.

Elderly persons encounter a variety of challenges as they age, and these challenges can impact their overall well-being and quality of life. Some common problems faced by elderly individuals include:

1. **Physical Health Issues:** Aging often brings about various health concerns, including chronic conditions, mobility issues, and a decline in overall physical well-being. Managing health conditions becomes a significant challenge for many elderly persons.
2. **Isolation and Loneliness:** Social isolation and loneliness are prevalent among the elderly, especially for those living alone or in care facilities. Loss of friends and family members, as well as limited mobility, can contribute to feelings of isolation.
3. **Financial Strain:** Elderly individuals may face financial difficulties due to factors such as retirement, fixed incomes, rising healthcare costs, and the need for long-term care. Financial constraints can limit their ability to access necessary resources and services.

4. **Cognitive Decline And Dementia:** Cognitive challenges, including memory loss and dementia, are common issues among the elderly. Alzheimer's disease and other forms of dementia pose significant challenges for both individuals and their caregivers.

5. **Elder Abuse:** Abuse, neglect, or exploitation of elderly individuals can occur in various settings, including homes, care facilities, or even by family members. This can have severe physical, emotional, and psychological consequences.

6. **Access to Healthcare:** Accessibility to quality healthcare can be a challenge, particularly in regions with limited resources or for those who face difficulties in transportation. Regular medical check-ups and timely access to healthcare services become crucial for maintaining well-being.

7. **Housing And Living Arrangements:** Elderly persons may encounter challenges related to housing, including accessibility issues, maintenance, and the need for modifications to make living spaces more age-friendly. Affordable and suitable housing options can be limited.

8. **Loss Of Independence:** With aging often comes a loss of independence, especially if there are mobility issues or health concerns. Maintaining a sense of autonomy and dignity becomes important for the well-being of elderly individuals.

9. **Technological Barriers:** The rapid advancement of technology can pose challenges for elderly persons who may face difficulties in adapting to new devices and digital communication methods. This can contribute to feelings of exclusion and a lack of access to information.

10. **End-Of-Life Planning:** Many elderly individuals may grapple with end-of-life decisions, including preferences for medical care, funeral arrangements, and legacy planning. These considerations can be emotionally challenging for both the individuals and their families.

Addressing the challenges faced by elderly persons requires a comprehensive and holistic approach, including social support networks, healthcare services, financial planning, and community initiatives to promote inclusivity and age-friendly environments. Providing resources and implementing policies that consider the unique needs of the elderly can contribute to improving their overall quality of life.

Psycho-Social Problems Among Differently-Abled Persons

- Differently-abled individuals often face significant psycho-social challenges, including societal stigma and discrimination that can contribute to feelings of isolation and low self-esteem.

- Accessibility issues pose a major concern, as physical barriers in public spaces and a lack of accommodations can limit the participation of differently-abled persons in various aspects of social life, exacerbating their sense of exclusion.

- Employment opportunities may be limited, leading to financial instability and dependence, which can impact their mental well-being and overall quality of life.

- Social attitudes and misconceptions about disabilities can create psychological stress, as differently-abled individuals may grapple with societal expectations and negative stereotypes, hindering their ability to form meaningful relationships.

- Additionally, inadequate mental health support and awareness exacerbate the psycho-social problems, highlighting the need for comprehensive strategies that address both the physical and mental well-being of differently-abled individuals to foster an inclusive and supportive society.

Problems Faced By Differently-Abled Elderly Persons

Differently-abled elderly persons often face a combination of challenges associated with aging and those related to their specific disabilities. These challenges can impact various aspects of their lives, and addressing them requires a nuanced and inclusive approach. Some common problems faced by differently-abled elderly individuals include:

1. **Limited Accessibility:** Elderly persons with disabilities may encounter barriers related to physical accessibility in public spaces, transportation, and housing. Lack of ramps, elevators, and accessible restrooms can restrict their mobility.

2. **Healthcare Disparities:** Access to appropriate healthcare services can be challenging for differently-abled elderly persons. Some may require specialized care, assistive devices, or accommodations that may not be readily available.

3. **Isolation And Loneliness:** Differently-abled elderly individuals may face heightened levels of isolation due to both age-related factors and the challenges associated with their disabilities. Limited social engagement and accessibility to community activities can contribute to loneliness.

4. **Financial Strain:** The costs associated with disabilities, such as assistive devices, home modifications, and specialized healthcare, can strain the finances of differently-abled elderly individuals. Limited financial resources may impact their ability to access necessary support.

5. **Caregiver Stress:** Family members or caregivers of differently-abled elderly persons may experience increased stress due to the additional responsibilities associated with providing care, assistance, and emotional support.

6. **Technological Gaps:** Rapid technological advancements may present challenges for differently-abled elderly individuals who may find it difficult to adapt to and use new assistive technologies. This can contribute to a digital divide, limiting their access to information and communication.

7. **Mental Health Concerns:** The intersection of aging and disability can contribute to mental health issues such as depression and anxiety. Coping with both the physical limitations of aging and the challenges posed by disabilities may require specialized mental health support.

8. **Abuse And Exploitation:** Vulnerability to abuse, neglect, or exploitation may be heightened for differently-abled elderly individuals. Issues such as financial exploitation or mistreatment in care facilities can pose significant risks.

9. **Transportation Challenges:** Accessible transportation becomes crucial for differently-abled elderly individuals to maintain independence and participate in community activities. Inadequate transportation options can limit their ability to move freely.

10. **Housing And Accommodation:** Finding suitable and accessible housing that meets the needs of differently-abled elderly individuals can be a considerable challenge. Modifications to living spaces may be necessary, but not all housing options may provide such accommodations.

Addressing the problems faced by differently-abled elderly persons requires a comprehensive and inclusive approach that considers both the aging process and the specific needs associated with different disabilities. This includes accessible infrastructure, healthcare services, social support systems, and policies that promote inclusivity and equality for all elderly individuals, regardless of their abilities.

Psychological Problems Of Disabled Adolescents And Young Adults

Disabled adolescents and young adults may face a range of psychological challenges that are unique to their experiences. It's important to recognize that each individual is unique, and the impact of disability on psychological well-being can vary widely. Here are some common psychological problems that disabled adolescents and young adults may encounter:

1. **Identity And Self-Esteem Issues:**
    - Disability can sometimes affect one's sense of identity and self-worth. Adolescents and young adults may struggle with accepting their disabilities and integrating them into their self-concept.

2. **Social Isolation:**
   - Disabled individuals may face challenges in socializing and forming connections, leading to feelings of isolation and loneliness. Social barriers and stigma can contribute to this isolation.

3. **Depression And Anxiety:**
   - Coping with a disability can be emotionally taxing, potentially leading to depression and anxiety. Concerns about the future, social acceptance, and the ability to lead a fulfilling life can contribute to these mental health challenges.

4. **Bullying And Stigmatization:**
   - Disabled individuals may be more susceptible to bullying and stigmatization, both of which can have a profound impact on mental health. Negative stereotypes and misconceptions about disabilities can contribute to discriminatory behavior.

5. **Educational Challenges:**
   - Access to education may be limited for some disabled individuals, leading to frustration, stress, and a sense of inadequacy. This can impact academic performance and future career opportunities.

6. **Family Dynamics:**
   - Family relationships may be affected as families navigate the challenges associated with disability. This can include strained communication, overprotection, or a lack of understanding, all of which can impact the mental well-being of the disabled individual.

7. **Adjustment Issues:**
   - Adolescents and young adults with disabilities may struggle with adapting to changes in their lives, whether related to their disability or other life transitions. This can lead to stress and difficulty coping with new situations.

8. **Chronic Pain And Health Concerns:**
   o Some disabilities come with chronic pain or health issues, which can contribute to psychological distress. Coping with ongoing physical discomfort can impact mental well-being.

9. **Limited Independence:**
   o Issues related to independence and autonomy may arise, especially if disabled individuals are dependent on others for daily activities. Striking a balance between independence and support can be challenging.

10. **Uncertain Future:**
    o Concerns about the future, including employment opportunities, relationships, and overall life satisfaction, may be heightened for disabled adolescents and young adults.

It's crucial to approach these challenges with a holistic and individualized perspective. Providing support, fostering a positive and inclusive environment, and addressing both the physical and psychological aspects of disability can contribute to better mental health outcomes for disabled individuals. Access to mental health services, peer support groups, and educational resources can also be valuable in addressing these psychological challenges.

Chapter 3
Continent-Wise Study

Challenges Faced By Differently-Abled Elderly Persons In Asian Continent And Its Sub-Continents

Differently-abled elderly persons in Asia and its sub-continents face a myriad of challenges, influenced by cultural, social, economic, and healthcare factors. The diversity within this vast region contributes to varying experiences for differently-abled individuals. Here are some common problems faced by differently-abled elderly persons in Asia and its sub-continents:

1. **Cultural Stigma And Discrimination:** Many Asian societies hold cultural beliefs and attitudes that may stigmatize or marginalize differently-abled individuals, leading to discrimination, social exclusion, and limited opportunities.

2. **Limited Accessibility:** Infrastructure in many Asian countries may not be fully accessible, with barriers in public spaces, transportation, and buildings. The lack of ramps, elevators, and accessible facilities hinders the mobility of differently-abled elderly persons.

3. **Healthcare Disparities:** Access to quality healthcare services can be uneven, particularly in rural areas. Differently-abled elderly individuals may face challenges in obtaining specialized care, assistive devices, and healthcare facilities with appropriate accessibility.

4. **Financial Strain:** Economic disparities and limited financial resources can impact differently-abled elderly persons' ability to access assistive devices, home modifications, and necessary support services, contributing to financial strain.

5. **Social Isolation:** Differently-abled elderly individuals may experience social isolation due to cultural perceptions, physical barriers, and a lack of awareness. This isolation can negatively impact their mental health and well-being.

6. **Family Care Responsibilities:** Asian cultures often place a strong emphasis on family care for elderly individuals. Differently-abled elderly persons may rely heavily on family members for support, potentially causing stress and strain on caregivers.

7. **Technological Gaps:** Rapid technological advancements may create a digital divide for differently-abled elderly individuals in Asia. Lack of access to and awareness of assistive technologies can limit their ability to stay connected and access information.

8. **Language And Communication Barriers:** In multicultural and multilingual societies in Asia, language barriers may pose challenges for differently-abled elderly persons in accessing healthcare, social services, and information about their rights and entitlements.

9. **Housing Challenges:** Finding suitable and accessible housing can be a significant challenge. Accessible housing options may be limited, especially in densely populated urban areas.

10. **Lack Of Inclusive Policies:** Some Asian countries may lack comprehensive and inclusive policies that address the specific needs of differently-abled elderly individuals. Advocacy for policy changes to promote accessibility and equal opportunities is crucial.

Here, India is taken for statistical study. In India, census has been done in the year 2011. As per census 2011 reports, the population of India was 121.08 crores and the population of disabled persons was 2.68 crores as shown in figure 1.

Population, India 2011			Disabled persons, India 2011		
Persons	Males	Females	Persons	Males	Females
121.08 crore	62.32 crore	58.76 crore	2.68 crore	1.50 crore	1.18 crore

Figure 1: Total population and population of the disabled persons in India-Census 2011 [1]

The Census 2011 revealed that, in India, 20% of the disabled persons are having disability in movement, 19% are with disability in seeing, 19 % are with disability in hearing and 8% has multiple disabilities as shown in figure 2.

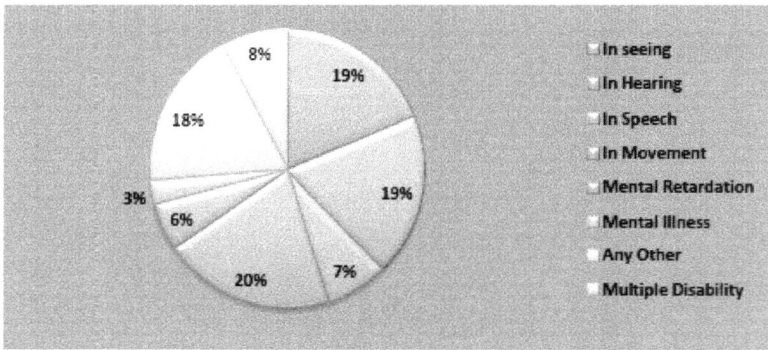

Figure 2: Disabled population by type of Disability in India - Census, 2011 [1]

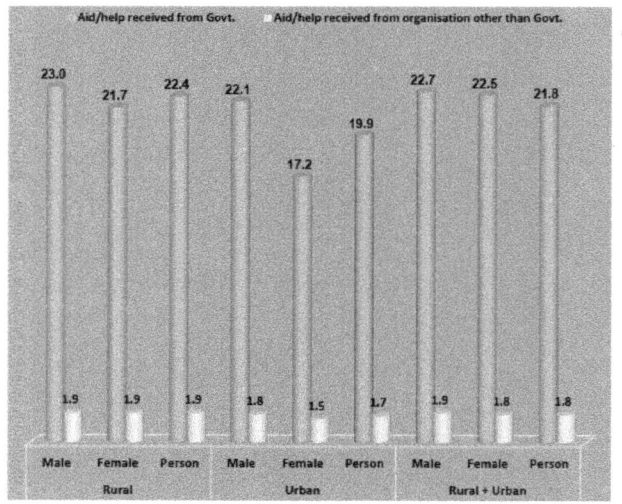

Figure 3: Percentage of person with disability who received any assistance-all-India [1]

Figure 3 show the percentage of disabled population in India received any kind of assistance from government of India and non-government organizations.

Addressing these challenges requires collaborative efforts involving governments, non-governmental organizations, communities, and healthcare providers. Cultural sensitivity, awareness campaigns, policy reforms, and investments in inclusive infrastructure are essential to improve the quality of life for differently-abled elderly persons in Asia and its sub-continents.

Challenges Faced By Differently-Abled Elderly Persons Across The Australian Continent And Its Sub-Continents

The challenges faced by differently-abled elderly persons across the Australian continent and its sub-continents (referring to the geographical region that includes Australia, New Zealand, and nearby islands) can vary due to cultural, economic, and regional differences. Here are some common problems faced by differently-abled elderly individuals in this region:

1. **Cultural Diversity:** The Australian continent and sub-continents comprise diverse cultures and Indigenous populations. Differently-abled elderly individuals from various cultural backgrounds may encounter unique challenges related to language, traditions, and cultural perceptions of disability.

2. **Accessibility Issues:** In both urban and rural areas, accessibility may vary. While major cities may have better infrastructure and facilities, rural and remote areas might lack accessible public spaces, transportation options, and healthcare services, impacting the mobility of differently-abled elderly persons.

3. **Indigenous Health Disparities:** Indigenous populations, such as Aboriginal and Torres Strait Islander peoples, may face specific health disparities, including higher rates of disability. Addressing the health and accessibility needs of differently-abled elderly individuals within Indigenous communities is crucial for achieving health equity.

4. **Healthcare Accessibility:** Access to healthcare services, particularly specialized care and assistive devices, can be a challenge. Differently-abled elderly individuals in remote areas may face difficulties accessing healthcare facilities, contributing to health disparities.

5. **Aging Population:** The Australian continent and sub-continents are experiencing an aging population, and this demographic shift poses challenges in providing adequate support and care for differently-abled elderly individuals, especially as the demand for services increases.

6. **Economic Disparities:** Economic factors can impact differently-abled elderly persons' access to essential resources, housing, and support services. Socioeconomic disparities may influence the level of care and assistance available to them.

7. **Social Inclusion:** Differently-abled elderly persons may face social isolation, particularly in communities where there is a lack of awareness and understanding about disabilities. Promoting social inclusion and combating stigma are essential for improving their quality of life.

8. **Legal Protections:** While there are legal protections against discrimination, enforcing these rights and ensuring equal opportunities for differently-abled elderly persons may require ongoing advocacy and awareness efforts, especially in diverse cultural contexts.

9. **Natural Disasters:** The Australian continent and nearby islands are prone to natural disasters such as bushfires, floods, and cyclones. Differently-abled elderly individuals may face increased vulnerability during such events, requiring special attention to disaster preparedness and response.

10. **Technology Divide:** The rapid technological advancements may create a digital divide for differently-abled elderly persons, especially in regions with limited access to technology. Ensuring digital inclusion is essential for their participation in online services and communication.

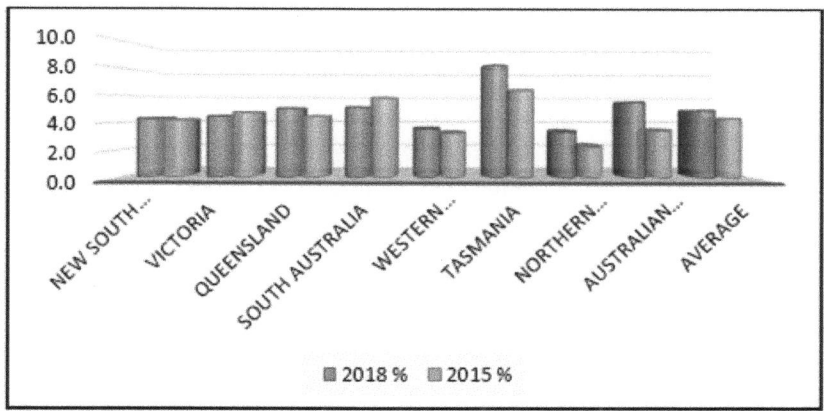

Figure 4: Persons with psychosocial disability, by state and territory of usual residence, 2018 and 2015 [3-7]

Figure 4 depicts the percentage of persons with psychosocial disabilities in different state and territories of Australia.

Addressing these challenges requires a multi-faceted approach involving governments, communities, advocacy groups, and healthcare providers. Tailoring solutions to the specific needs of differently-abled elderly individuals in diverse cultural and geographical contexts is essential for promoting inclusivity and improving their overall well-being.

Challenges Faced By Differently-Abled Elderly Persons In Africa And Its Sub-Continents

Differently-abled elderly persons in Africa and its sub-continents face a unique set of challenges influenced by diverse cultural, economic, and healthcare factors. The following are some common problems faced by differently-abled elderly individuals in these regions:

1. **Healthcare Disparities:** Access to quality healthcare services can be challenging in many African countries. Differently-abled elderly individuals may face difficulties obtaining specialized care, assistive devices, and appropriate medical facilities.

2. **Limited Accessibility:** Infrastructure in some African countries may lack accessibility features, including ramps, elevators, and adapted transportation, making it difficult for differently-abled elderly persons to move around and access public spaces.

3. **Cultural Stigma And Discrimination:** Cultural beliefs and practices may contribute to stigma and discrimination against differently-abled individuals. This can result in social exclusion, limiting opportunities for employment, education, and social participation.

4. **Economic Challenges:** Economic disparities and poverty in certain regions of Africa can exacerbate the difficulties faced by differently-abled elderly individuals. Limited financial resources may impact their ability to access assistive devices, healthcare, and support services.

5. **Social Isolation:** Differently-abled elderly persons may experience social isolation due to cultural perceptions, a lack of awareness, and inadequate social support systems. Loneliness can have detrimental effects on mental health.

6. **Educational Barriers:** Limited accessibility and accommodations in educational institutions may restrict the opportunities for differently-abled elderly individuals to access lifelong learning, skill development, and social engagement.

7. **Inadequate Social Support Services:** In some regions, there may be insufficient social support services, including counseling, mental health services, and community programs that address the unique needs of differently-abled elderly individuals.

8. **Technological Gaps:** The digital divide may impact differently-abled elderly persons in Africa, limiting their access to information, communication, and assistive technologies that could enhance their quality of life.

9. **Housing Challenges:** Finding suitable and accessible housing can be difficult. Accessible infrastructure and housing options may be limited, especially in rural areas.

10. **Natural Disasters And Humanitarian Crises:** Differently-abled elderly persons may be disproportionately affected by natural disasters and humanitarian crises due to challenges in evacuation, lack of accessible shelters, and disruptions to support services.

Addressing these challenges requires collaborative efforts from governments, non-governmental organizations, communities, and international agencies. Culturally sensitive approaches, awareness campaigns, policy reforms, and investments in inclusive infrastructure are crucial to improving the well-being of differently-abled elderly persons in Africa and its sub-continents.

Challenges Faced By Differently-Abled Elderly Persons In North America Continent And Its Sub-Continents

In North America, which primarily includes countries like the United States and Canada, differently-abled elderly persons face challenges that can vary based on factors such as cultural diversity, healthcare systems, and regional variations. Below are some common problems faced by differently-abled elderly individuals in North America and its sub-continents:

1. **Healthcare Costs:** The high costs associated with healthcare, including specialized services, medications, and assistive devices, can pose a significant challenge for differently-abled elderly individuals, especially if they are on fixed incomes.

2. **Accessibility Issues:** While many urban areas have made progress in terms of accessibility, some regions may still have challenges related to accessible public spaces, transportation, and buildings, affecting the mobility of differently-abled elderly persons.

3. **Social Isolation:** Differently-abled elderly individuals may experience social isolation, particularly if they face physical barriers or encounter age-related discrimination. Social support services are crucial to addressing loneliness and fostering a sense of community.

4. **Legal Protections:** Although there are legal protections against discrimination, enforcing these rights and ensuring equal opportunities for differently-abled elderly persons may require ongoing advocacy and awareness efforts.

5. **Housing Challenges:** Accessible and affordable housing options can be limited, particularly in densely populated urban areas. Differently-abled elderly individuals may face difficulties finding suitable living arrangements.

6. **Technological Gaps:** The rapid evolution of technology may create a digital divide for differently-abled elderly individuals, impacting their access to information, online services, and assistive technologies.

7. **Transportation Issues:** Accessible transportation options are essential for differently-abled elderly individuals to maintain independence and participate in community activities. Challenges may arise in regions with limited public transportation or inadequate accessibility features.

8. **Employment Opportunities:** Differently-abled elderly individuals may face challenges in accessing employment opportunities due to ageism and perceptions about their abilities. This can lead to financial strain and limited financial resources.

9. **Mental Health Concerns:** Coping with disabilities, age-related changes, and potential social isolation can contribute to mental health issues. Access to mental health services and community support is crucial for the well-being of differently-abled elderly individuals.

10. **Caregiver Support:** Family members or caregivers of differently-abled elderly persons may experience stress and burnout due to the responsibilities associated with providing care, assistance, and emotional support.

Addressing these challenges involves a multi-faceted approach, including the implementation of inclusive policies, increased accessibility, community support programs, and efforts to combat ageism and discrimination. Collaborative initiatives from governments, advocacy groups, and communities can contribute to creating a more inclusive and supportive environment for differently-abled elderly persons in North America and its sub-continents.

Challenges Faced By Differently-Abled Elderly Persons In South America Continent And Its Sub-Continents

Differently-abled elderly persons in South America and its sub-continents face a range of challenges influenced by cultural, economic, and healthcare factors. Here are some common problems faced by differently-abled elderly individuals in this region:

1. **Healthcare Disparities:** Access to quality healthcare services can be uneven across South America. Differently-abled elderly persons may encounter challenges in obtaining specialized care, assistive devices, and healthcare facilities with appropriate accessibility.

2. **Economic Disparities:** Economic inequalities can impact differently-abled elderly persons' ability to access essential resources, including assistive devices, healthcare, and support services. Limited financial resources may contribute to financial strain.

3. **Limited Accessibility:** Infrastructure in some South American countries may lack accessibility features, hindering the mobility of differently-abled elderly persons in public spaces, transportation, and buildings.

4. **Cultural Stigma And Discrimination:** Cultural attitudes towards disabilities may contribute to stigma and discrimination, limiting social inclusion and opportunities for differently-abled elderly individuals.

5. **Social Isolation:** Differently-abled elderly individuals may experience social isolation due to cultural perceptions, physical barriers, and a lack of awareness. Loneliness can negatively impact mental health and overall well-being.

6. **Educational Barriers:** Limited accessibility and accommodations in educational institutions may restrict the opportunities for differently-abled elderly individuals to access lifelong learning, skill development, and social engagement.

7. **Family Care Responsibilities:** In South American cultures, there is often an emphasis on family care for elderly individuals. Differently-abled elderly persons may rely heavily on family members for support, potentially causing stress and strain on caregivers.

8. **Technological Gaps:** The digital divide may impact differently-abled elderly persons in South America, limiting their access to information, communication, and assistive technologies that could enhance their quality of life.

9. **Housing Challenges:** Finding suitable and accessible housing can be a significant challenge. Accessible infrastructure and housing options may be limited, especially in rural areas.

10. **Legal Protections:** While some South American countries have legal protections against discrimination, enforcing these rights and ensuring equal opportunities for differently-abled elderly persons may require ongoing advocacy and awareness efforts.

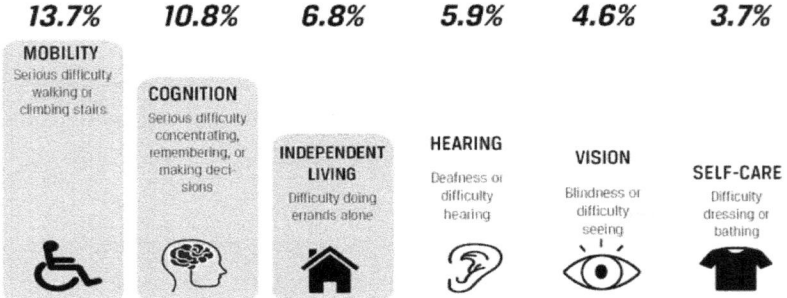

Figure 5: Functional disabilities status in the United States of America [2]

Figure 1 shows that in the United States of America, Mobility is the highest among all other categories of the functional disabilities. Addressing these challenges involves collaborative efforts from governments, non-governmental organizations, communities, and healthcare providers. Cultural sensitivity, awareness campaigns, policy reforms, and investments in inclusive infrastructure are crucial to improving the well-being of differently-abled elderly persons in South America and its sub-continents.

Challenges Faced By Differently-Abled Elderly Persons In Antarctica Continent And Its Sub-Continents

Till January 2023, Antarctica is a continent largely uninhabited by a permanent human population, and it does not have sub-continents. The Antarctic Treaty System, which designates Antarctica as a scientific preserve, prohibits military activity, mineral mining, and nuclear testing, and it supports scientific research. Due to its extreme climate and lack of permanent settlements, the continent poses unique challenges for any population, including differently-abled individuals.

In the unlikely scenario of differently-abled elderly persons being present in Antarctica (such as researchers or support staff involved in scientific activities), potential challenges might include:

1. **Harsh Environmental Conditions:** Antarctica has extreme weather conditions with extremely low temperatures, strong winds, and limited sunlight during winter. Differently-abled individuals may face additional difficulties in navigating these harsh conditions.

2. **Limited Infrastructure:** The continent has minimal infrastructure, and facilities are primarily designed for scientific research. Accessibility features may be limited, and mobility could be a challenge for differently-abled individuals.

3. **Isolation And Limited Medical Facilities:** Antarctica is isolated from the rest of the world, and medical facilities are limited. Differently-abled elderly persons may face challenges in accessing specialized healthcare services and support.

4. **Transportation Challenges:** Travel to and from Antarctica involves long and challenging journeys, often by sea or air. Accessible transportation options may be limited, and the remote location can exacerbate the difficulties for differently-abled individuals.

5. **Extreme Terrain:** The terrain in Antarctica is rugged and icy, posing challenges for individuals with mobility issues. Navigating uneven surfaces and icy conditions may be particularly difficult for differently-abled elderly persons.

It's important to note that the population in Antarctica is generally limited to scientists, support staff, and researchers, and these individuals undergo rigorous medical and physical assessments before participating in expeditions. The unique challenges of Antarctica, combined with its extreme conditions and limited infrastructure, make it an environment that requires careful planning and consideration for the well-being of all individuals, including those with disabilities.

Challenges Faced By Differently-Abled Elderly Persons In European Continent And Its Sub-Continents

In the European continent and its sub-continents, differently-abled elderly persons encounter various challenges that can impact their daily lives and overall well-being. The specific problems faced by these individuals may vary across different countries and regions, but some common issues include:

1. **Healthcare Disparities:** Access to quality healthcare services may vary across European countries. Differently-abled elderly individuals may face challenges in obtaining specialized care, assistive devices, and accessible healthcare facilities.

2. **Accessibility Issues:** While many European countries have made progress in terms of accessibility, there can still be challenges related to accessible public spaces, transportation, and buildings. Limited accessibility can hinder the mobility of differently-abled elderly persons.

3. **Social Inclusion:** Differently-abled elderly individuals may experience social isolation due to physical barriers, a lack of awareness, and potential age-related discrimination. Promoting social inclusion and community engagement is essential for their well-being.

4. **Economic Challenges:** Economic factors, such as limited financial resources and pension disparities, can impact differently-abled elderly persons' ability to access essential resources, including assistive devices and support services.

5. **Housing Challenges:** Accessible and affordable housing options may be limited, especially in urban areas. Differently-abled elderly individuals may face difficulties finding suitable living arrangements that meet their accessibility needs.

6. **Employment Opportunities:** Ageism and perceptions about abilities can present challenges for differently-abled elderly persons seeking employment or participating in the workforce. Limited employment opportunities can contribute to financial strain.

7. **Technological Gaps:** Rapid technological advancements may create a digital divide, impacting differently-abled elderly individuals' access to information, online services, and assistive technologies that could enhance their quality of life.

8. **Transportation Issues:** Accessible transportation options are crucial for differently-abled elderly persons to maintain independence and participate in community activities. Challenges may arise in regions with limited public transportation or inadequate accessibility features.

9. **Legal Protections:** While many European countries have legal protections against discrimination, enforcing these rights and ensuring equal opportunities for differently-abled elderly persons may require ongoing advocacy and awareness efforts.

10. **Caregiver Support:** Family members or caregivers of differently-abled elderly persons may experience stress and burnout due to the responsibilities associated with providing care, assistance, and emotional support.

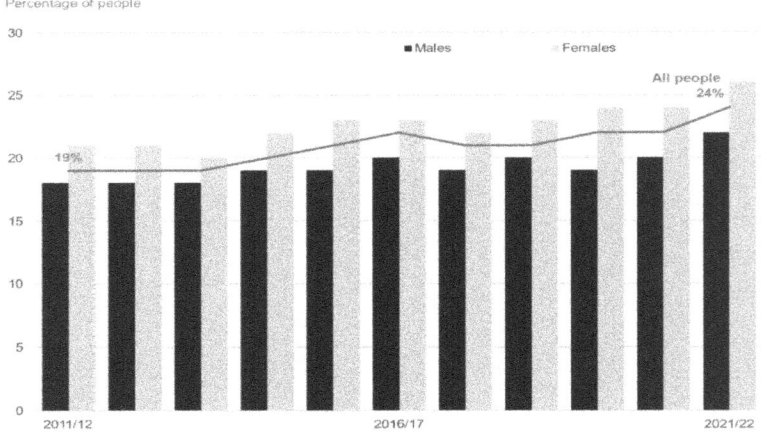

Figure 6: Percentage of disabled people by gender, financial year ending 2012 to financial year ending 2022, United Kingdom [8]

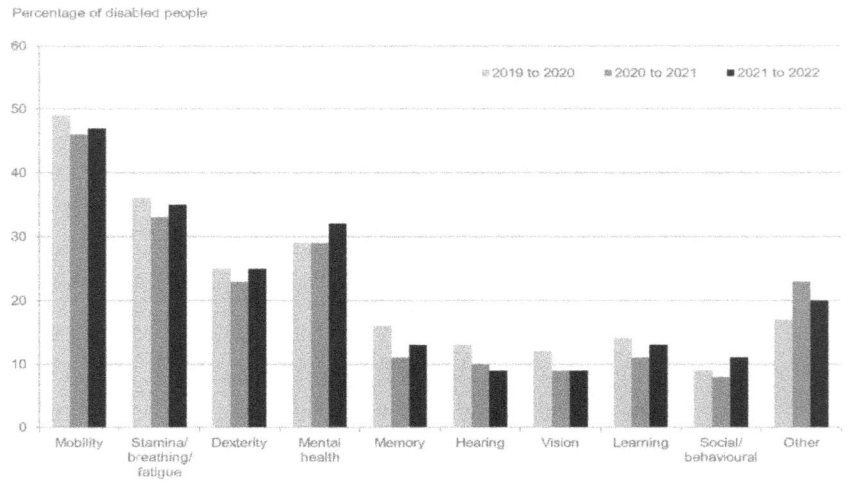

Figure 7: Percentage of disabled people by impairment types, 2019 to 2020, 2020 to 2021 and 2021 to 2022, United Kingdom [8]

Figure 6 and 7 shows the percentage of disabled persons in the United Kingdom and their impairment types, respectively.

Addressing these challenges necessitates collaborative efforts from governments, non-governmental organizations, communities, and healthcare providers. The implementation of inclusive policies, increased accessibility, community support programs, and efforts to combat ageism and discrimination are crucial to improving the well-being of differently-abled elderly persons in the European continent and its sub-continents.

Chapter 4
Issues And Government Policies

Issues With Steps Taken By Government On Problems Faced By The Differently-Abled Elderly Persons

The issues faced by differently-abled elderly persons often revolve around accessibility, social inclusion, healthcare, and financial support. Governments worldwide have implemented various steps to address these challenges, but there can still be several issues that need attention and improvement. Here are some common problems associated with the steps taken by governments:

1. **Inadequate Accessibility:**
   - **Physical Infrastructure:** Many places lack proper infrastructure such as ramps, elevators, and accessible transportation, making it difficult for differently-abled elderly individuals to move around independently.
   - **Digital Accessibility:** The increasing reliance on digital platforms for services may create barriers for those with disabilities if websites and online services are not designed with accessibility in mind.

2. **Insufficient Social Inclusion:**
   - **Community Engagement:** There may be a lack of programs and initiatives to encourage social inclusion and participation of differently-abled elderly individuals in community activities.
   - **Stigma And Discrimination:** Negative attitudes and stereotypes can contribute to the exclusion of these individuals from social and recreational opportunities.

3. **Healthcare Challenges:**
   - **Limited Access To Healthcare Services:** Differently-abled elderly persons may face challenges in accessing healthcare facilities that are equipped to meet their specific needs.
   - **Affordability:** Healthcare costs, especially for specialized care and assistive devices, can be a significant financial burden for individuals and their families.

4. **Financial Support:**
   - **Inadequate Financial Assistance:** Government assistance programs may not provide sufficient financial support to cover the additional expenses associated with disabilities, such as medical costs, assistive devices, and caregiving services.
   - **Complex Application Processes:** Complicated and time-consuming application processes for disability benefits can discourage eligible individuals from seeking the support they need.

5. **Education And Employment Opportunities:**
   - **Limited Access to Education:** Differently-abled elderly individuals may face barriers in accessing education and training programs that can enhance their skills and employability.
   - **Discrimination In The Workplace:** Employment discrimination based on age and disability can limit job opportunities for the elderly, exacerbating financial challenges.

6. **Inadequate Policy Implementation:**
   - **Lack of Enforcement:** Even when supportive policies are in place, inadequate enforcement mechanisms may lead to non-compliance and a lack of accountability among businesses and organizations.
   - **Policy Gaps:** Some policies may not comprehensively address the unique needs of differently-abled elderly individuals, leading to gaps in support.

Addressing these issues requires a holistic approach, including improved policy frameworks, increased awareness, community engagement, and collaboration between government, non-profit organizations, and the private sector. Regular assessments and updates to policies based on feedback from the affected community can help ensure that the steps taken by the government are effective in addressing the challenges faced by differently-abled elderly persons.

Till January 2022, following steps taken by the Australian government for differently-abled individuals, including the elderly. Keep in mind that policies and initiatives may have evolved since then, and it's advisable to check the latest government sources for the most up-to-date information. Here are some common measures and programs that the Australian government has historically implemented:

1. **National Disability Insurance Scheme (NDIS):**
   o The NDIS is a significant initiative designed to provide support and services to people with disabilities, including elderly individuals. It aims to empower individuals with disabilities to achieve their goals and participate in community life.

2. **Aged Care Services:**
   o The Australian government provides various aged care services, including support for elderly individuals with disabilities. This may include home care services, residential care, and respite care to assist both the elderly and their caregivers.

3. **Disability Discrimination Act (DDA):**
   o The DDA is a legislative framework in Australia that promotes equal rights and opportunities for people with disabilities. It covers various areas, including employment, education, and access to goods and services.

4. **Accessible Public Spaces:**
   o Efforts have been made to improve the accessibility of public spaces and infrastructure. This includes the provision of ramps, accessible transportation, and facilities that cater to the needs of individuals with disabilities, including the elderly.

5. **Support For Careers:**
   o The Australian government recognizes the role of caregivers and provides support services, including financial assistance and respite care, to those caring for elderly individuals with disabilities.

6. **Assistive Technology And Equipment:**
   o Various programs and funding initiatives exist to support the acquisition of assistive technology and equipment that can enhance the independence and quality of life for differently-abled elderly individuals.

7. **Disability Employment Services:**
   o Programs are in place to support individuals with disabilities, including the elderly, in gaining and maintaining employment. This includes tailored employment services and support for workplace accommodations.

8. **Accessible Housing Initiatives:**
   o There have been initiatives to promote accessible housing, ensuring that homes are designed to accommodate the needs of individuals with disabilities, including the elderly.

9. **Healthcare Access:**
   o Access to healthcare services is a priority, and efforts are made to ensure that healthcare facilities are equipped to meet the needs of individuals with disabilities. This includes accessible medical facilities and services.

10. **Community Inclusion Programs:**
    o Various community inclusion programs and initiatives aim to enhance social participation and reduce isolation among differently-abled elderly individuals.

It's important to note that the Australian government regularly reviews and updates policies related to disability support, and new initiatives may have been introduced.

Steps Taken By Indian Government For Differently-Abled Elderly Persons

Till January 2022, the Indian government has implemented various measures to support differently-abled individuals, including the elderly. However, policies and programs may evolve, and it's advisable to check the latest government sources for the most up-to-date information. Here are some steps and initiatives that the Indian government has historically taken:

1. **Rights Of Persons With Disabilities Act (RPWD), 2016:**
   o The RPWD Act replaced the Persons with Disabilities (Equal Opportunities, Protection of Rights and Full Participation) Act, 1995, and is aimed at safeguarding the rights of persons with disabilities, including the elderly. It provides a legal framework for equality, non-discrimination, and inclusion.

2. **National Social Assistance Programme (NSAP):**
   o The NSAP includes the Indira Gandhi National Disability Pension Scheme (IGNDPS), which provides financial assistance to persons with disabilities, including elderly individuals, who are below the poverty line.

3. **Accessible India Campaign (Sugamya Bharat Abhiyan):**
   o Launched as part of the Swachh Bharat Abhiyan, this campaign aims to make public spaces, transportation, and information accessible to persons with disabilities, including the elderly. It focuses on creating a barrier-free environment.

4. **National Institute Of Social Defence (NISD):**
   o The NISD works on various aspects related to the welfare of vulnerable groups, including differently-abled individuals and the elderly. It is involved in training, research, and capacity-building programs.

5. **Integrated Programme For Older Persons (IPOP):**
   o IPOP is a centrally sponsored scheme that supports various welfare programs for the elderly, including those with disabilities. It includes components related to healthcare, financial assistance, and awareness generation.

6. **Assistance To Disabled Persons For Purchase/Fitting Of Aids And Appliances (ADIP):**
   - This scheme provides financial assistance to differently-abled individuals for the purchase of aids and appliances to promote their physical, social, and psychological rehabilitation.

7. **Accessible Voting:**
   - Efforts have been made to make the voting process more accessible for differently-abled individuals, including the elderly. This includes providing facilities such as ramps and accessible voting machines.

8. **Inclusive Education:**
   - The government has emphasized inclusive education, aiming to provide equal opportunities for education to children and individuals with disabilities, irrespective of their age.

9. **Rashtriya Vayoshri Yojana:**
   - Launched by the Ministry of Social Justice and Empowerment, this scheme provides free physical aids and assistive living devices to senior citizens belonging to BPL (Below Poverty Line) category.

10. **National Action Plan For Senior Citizens (Napsrc):**
    - The NAPSrC focuses on the overall welfare of senior citizens, including those with disabilities. It covers healthcare, financial security, and social integration.

It's important to note that these initiatives represent a snapshot of government efforts, and there may be additional programs and policies at the state level.

Steps Taken By The United States Government For Differently-Abled Elderly Persons

The United States government has implemented various measures to support differently-abled individuals, including the elderly. Please note that policies and programs may have evolved since then, and it's advisable to check the latest government sources for the most up-to-date information. Here are some key steps and initiatives taken by the American government:

1. **Americans With Disabilities Act (ADA):**
   - Enacted in 1990, the ADA is a comprehensive civil rights law that prohibits discrimination against individuals with disabilities. It covers various areas, including employment, public services, public accommodations, and telecommunications.

2. **Older Americans Act (OAA):**
   - The OAA provides funding and support for a range of services that benefit older Americans, including those with disabilities. Programs include nutrition services, caregiver support, and preventive health services.

3. **Social Security Disability Insurance (SSDI):**
   - SSDI provides financial support to individuals with disabilities, including elderly individuals, who have contributed to Social Security through payroll taxes and are no longer able to work due to a qualifying disability.

4. **Supplemental Security Income (SSI):**
   - SSI is a needs-based program that provides financial assistance to elderly individuals and individuals with disabilities who have limited income and resources.

5. **Medicare:**
   - Medicare is a federal health insurance program primarily for individuals aged 65 and older, but it also covers certain individuals with disabilities. It provides coverage for hospital stays, medical services, and prescription drugs.

6. **Medicaid:**
   - Medicaid is a joint federal and state program that provides health coverage to low-income individuals, including elderly individuals and those with disabilities. It covers a broad range of services, including long-term care.

7. **Accessible Housing Initiatives:**
   - Various federal programs and initiatives aim to promote accessible housing for individuals with disabilities, including the elderly. This includes grants and resources for home modifications.

8. **Transportation Accessibility:**
   - The U.S. Department of Transportation works to ensure accessible transportation for individuals with disabilities, including elderly individuals. This includes regulations for accessible public transit and infrastructure.

9. **Employment Programs:**
   - The U.S. Department of Labor has programs and initiatives to promote the employment of individuals with disabilities. This includes vocational rehabilitation services and efforts to increase workplace accessibility.

10. **National Institute On Aging (NIA):**
    - The NIA, part of the National Institutes of Health (NIH), conducts and supports research on aging, including research that addresses the unique needs of older individuals with disabilities.

These are just a few examples of the steps taken by the U.S. government to support differently-abled elderly individuals. There are additional programs at the federal, state, and local levels that provide assistance and services.

Steps Taken By The Europeon Government For Differently-Abled Elderly Persons

European governments have implemented various measures to support differently-abled elderly persons. However, it's important to note that policies and initiatives may evolve, and new developments may have occurred since then. Here are some general steps that European governments typically take to support differently-abled elderly individuals:

1. **Social Security And Pension Systems:**
   - European countries often have robust social security and pension systems to provide financial support to elderly individuals, including those with disabilities.

2. **Healthcare Services:**
   - Accessible and affordable healthcare services are essential for differently-abled elderly persons. European countries usually strive to provide comprehensive healthcare, including specialized services for individuals with disabilities.

3. **Inclusive Housing Policies:**
   - Governments promote inclusive housing policies, ensuring that housing options are accessible and accommodating for differently-abled individuals. This may include adapting existing housing or creating new accessible housing units.

4. **Transportation Accessibility:**
   - European governments work to make public transportation systems more accessible for individuals with disabilities, including the elderly. This involves providing accessible vehicles, infrastructure, and services.

5. **Employment Support:**
   - Programs and policies are often in place to support differently-abled elderly individuals in the workforce. This may include vocational training, workplace accommodations, and incentives for employers to hire individuals with disabilities.

6. **Education And Training:**
   - Continuing education and training opportunities are crucial for maintaining the independence and well-being of differently-abled elderly persons. European governments may implement programs to ensure access to lifelong learning.

7. **Social Inclusion Programs:**
   - Governments support initiatives that promote social inclusion and prevent isolation among differently-abled elderly individuals. This can include community centers, social activities, and support groups.

8. **Legal Protections And Anti-Discrimination Laws:**
   - European countries typically have laws in place to protect the rights of individuals with disabilities, including the elderly. Anti-discrimination laws aim to ensure equal opportunities in various aspects of life.

9. **Technology And Assistive Devices:**
   - Governments may invest in research and development of assistive technologies to enhance the independence and quality of life for differently-abled elderly individuals.

10. **Care And Support Services:**
    - There are often support services and caregiving programs in place to assist differently-abled elderly persons in their daily activities, both at home and in care facilities.

Steps Taken By The African Government For Differently-Abled Elderly Persons

Support for differently-abled elderly persons in Africa varies significantly from one country to another due to the continent's diversity and the differing levels of economic and social development. Following are some general steps that African governments may take to support differently-abled elderly individuals:

1. **Social Assistance Programs:**
   - Some African countries have social assistance programs that provide financial support to elderly individuals, including those with disabilities. These programs may include pensions, grants, or subsidies to help meet basic needs.

2. **Healthcare Services:**
   - Access to healthcare is crucial for differently-abled elderly individuals. Governments may work to ensure that healthcare services are accessible and affordable, with a focus on meeting the specific healthcare needs of individuals with disabilities.

3. **Community-Based Rehabilitation Programs:**
   - Some countries implement community-based rehabilitation programs to provide healthcare, education, and vocational training services at the community level. These programs may benefit differently-abled elderly individuals by promoting inclusion and enhancing their quality of life.

4. **Accessible Infrastructure:**
   - Governments may invest in creating accessible infrastructure, including public buildings, transportation, and public spaces. This can improve mobility and independence for differently-abled individuals, including the elderly.

5. **Inclusive Education Initiatives:**
   - Inclusive education policies aim to provide educational opportunities for differently-abled individuals, fostering an environment that supports their learning and development. This may include special education programs and accessible facilities.

6. **Employment Support:**
   - Policies and programs may be in place to support differently-abled individuals, including the elderly, in the workforce. This can include vocational training, job placement services, and incentives for employers to hire individuals with disabilities.

7. **Awareness And Sensitization Campaigns:**
   - Governments may conduct awareness campaigns to promote understanding and acceptance of differently-abled individuals in society. These campaigns can help reduce stigma and discrimination.

8. **Legal Protections:**
   - Some African countries have laws and policies in place to protect the rights of individuals with disabilities, including the elderly. These laws may address issues such as accessibility, discrimination, and the right to participate fully in society.

9. **NGO And Civil Society Involvement:**
   - Non-governmental organizations (NGOs) and civil society play a significant role in providing support to differently-abled elderly individuals. Governments may collaborate with these organizations to implement programs and initiatives.

10. **Assistive Technologies:**
    - Access to assistive technologies can greatly enhance the independence and quality of life for differently-abled elderly individuals. Governments may work to promote the availability and affordability of such technologies.

Solution To Psycho-Social Problems Among Differently-Abled Persons

Addressing psycho-social problems among differently-abled persons requires a comprehensive and inclusive approach that considers their unique needs and challenges. Here are some strategies and solutions:

1. **Community Education And Awareness:**
   - Conduct awareness campaigns to educate the community about different types of disabilities, reduce stigma, and promote understanding. This can contribute to creating a more inclusive and supportive environment.

2. **Counseling And Mental Health Support:**
   - Provide accessible counseling services and mental health support tailored to the needs of differently-abled individuals. This may involve training counselors to understand the specific challenges faced by this population.

3. **Peer Support Programs:**
   - Establish peer support networks where differently-abled individuals can connect with others facing similar challenges. Peer support can provide a sense of belonging, shared experiences, and practical advice.

4. **Inclusive Education Programs:**
   - Implement and promote inclusive education programs that accommodate the diverse learning needs of differently-abled

individuals. Inclusive environments foster social integration and reduce feelings of isolation.

5. **Skill Development And Employment Opportunities:**
    o Create vocational training programs that equip differently-abled individuals with skills for employment. Access to meaningful employment can enhance self-esteem and socio-economic well-being.

6. **Accessible Recreational Activities:**
    o Ensure that recreational and social activities are accessible to differently-abled individuals. This promotes social interaction, physical well-being, and a sense of inclusion within the community.

7. **Adaptive Technologies:**
    o Facilitate access to adaptive technologies and tools that empower differently-abled individuals to communicate, work, and engage with the world. Technology can enhance independence and social participation.

8. **Advocacy For Rights And Inclusion:**
    o Support advocacy initiatives that promote the rights of differently-abled individuals and advocate for inclusive policies in education, employment, and public spaces.

9. **Family Support Programs:**
    o Offer programs that provide support and resources for families of differently-abled individuals. Family support is crucial for the overall well-being of the individual and can contribute to a more supportive environment.

10. **Accessible Transportation:**
    o Improve accessibility in transportation systems to ensure that differently-abled individuals can participate in community activities and have the freedom to move independently.

11. **Government Policies And Legislation:**
    o Advocate for and implement policies and legislation that protect the rights of differently-abled individuals and promote their inclusion in all aspects of society.

12. Capacity Building For Professionals:
- Provide training for healthcare professionals, educators, and social workers to better understand and address the psycho-social needs of differently-abled individuals.

13. Promotion Of Cultural Sensitivity:
- Encourage cultural sensitivity in communities to ensure that cultural norms and practices do not hinder the social inclusion of differently-abled individuals.

14. Regular Assessments and Monitoring:
- Establish mechanisms for regular assessments and monitoring of psycho-social well-being among differently-abled individuals to identify and address emerging challenges promptly.

Chapter 5
A Fictional Case Study

A Fictional Case Study To Illustrate The Application Of Psycho-Social Support For A Differently-Abled Individual

Case Study: Emma's Journey to Empowerment

Background: Emma, a 35-year-old woman, has been differently-abled since childhood due to a congenital condition affecting her mobility. Despite her physical challenges, Emma is a highly intelligent and motivated individual. She has faced various psycho-social difficulties, including social isolation, employment discrimination, and struggles with self-esteem.

Presenting Issues: Emma recently completed her education, earning a degree in computer science. However, she has faced numerous challenges in securing employment due to misconceptions about her abilities. Emma is feeling frustrated, isolated, and her self-esteem is at a low point.

Intervention

1. Counseling and Support: Emma is connected with a psycho-social support team that includes a counselor, a career advisor, and a disability rights advocate. The counselor helps Emma address her feelings of frustration and isolation, working on strategies to enhance her self-esteem and resilience.

2. Career Development: The career advisor conducts a comprehensive assessment of Emma's skills and interests. Together, they identify job opportunities that align with her qualifications. The advisor also collaborates with potential employers to raise awareness about the benefits of workplace diversity and accommodations.

3. **Community Inclusion:** Emma is encouraged to participate in community events and support groups for differently-abled individuals. This fosters a sense of belonging and provides her with a supportive network that understands her challenges. Emma becomes an active member of a local disability advocacy group.

4. **Skill Enhancement:** Recognizing Emma's passion for technology, the support team facilitates additional training in accessible software development and assistive technologies. This not only enhances Emma's skill set but also positions her as a valuable asset in the job market.

5. **Advocacy for Inclusivity:** The disability rights advocate works with local businesses and organizations to promote inclusivity and diversity. Emma shares her experiences at awareness events, challenging stereotypes and advocating for equal opportunities for differently-abled individuals.

Outcome

Over time, Emma's journey is marked by significant progress. She secures a fulfilling job at a tech company that values diversity and provides reasonable accommodations. Her involvement in community advocacy not only empowers her but also contributes to positive changes in societal attitudes toward differently-abled individuals.

This case study emphasizes the importance of a holistic psycho-social support approach, including counseling, career development, community inclusion, skill enhancement, and advocacy, to empower differently-abled individuals and foster a more inclusive and supportive society.

The World Programme Of Action Concerning Disabled Persons

The World Programme of Action Concerning Disabled Persons is a comprehensive international framework aimed at promoting equalization of opportunities, rehabilitation, and full participation of people with disabilities in all aspects of life. Adopted by the United Nations General Assembly in 1982, this program outlines key principles and strategies for addressing the rights and needs of persons with disabilities. The World Programme of Action is instrumental in guiding national policies and international cooperation to ensure the inclusion and well-being of individuals with disabilities. Here are some key aspects of the World Programme of Action Concerning Disabled Persons:

Equalization Of Opportunities

The program emphasizes the need to eliminate discrimination and ensure equal opportunities for persons with disabilities in various spheres of life, including education, employment, and social participation.

Rehabilitation And Support Services

Rehabilitation services play a crucial role in enabling individuals with disabilities to achieve their full potential. The program highlights the importance of providing comprehensive rehabilitation services, including medical, social, and vocational support.

Prevention Of Disabilities

Recognizing the importance of prevention, the program advocates for measures to minimize the occurrence of disabilities, especially those that are preventable through health interventions, safety measures, and public health campaigns.

Accessibility And Integration

The World Programme of Action emphasizes the creation of accessible environments and the integration of persons with disabilities into mainstream society. This includes promoting accessible infrastructure, transportation, and communication.

Participation In Decision-Making

People with disabilities should have the opportunity to participate actively in decision-making processes that affect their lives. The program encourages the inclusion of individuals with disabilities in policy development and implementation.

Research And Data Collection

The program recognizes the importance of research and data collection to better understand the needs and experiences of individuals with disabilities. This information is crucial for developing evidence-based policies and programs.

International Cooperation

International cooperation is essential for addressing the global challenges faced by persons with disabilities. The program calls for collaboration between countries, organizations, and stakeholders to share knowledge, resources, and best practices.

Human Rights Perspective

The World Programme of Action is aligned with the broader human rights framework. It emphasizes the rights of persons with disabilities, including the right to equality, non-discrimination, and full participation in social, economic, and cultural life.

Implementation At The National Level

Member states are encouraged to develop and implement national policies and programs that align with the principles outlined in the World Programme of Action. This involves incorporating disability-related considerations into various sectors of governance.

Monitoring And Evaluation

Regular monitoring and evaluation mechanisms are essential to assess the progress made in the implementation of the program. This ensures accountability and provides an opportunity for adjustments to be made based on evolving needs and challenges.

The World Programme of Action Concerning Disabled Persons represents a significant international commitment to promoting the rights and well-being of individuals with disabilities. It serves as a guiding framework for countries to develop inclusive policies and practices that empower persons with disabilities to participate fully in society.

Psychological And Social Aspects Of Disability

The psychological and social aspects of disability encompass a complex interplay of individual experiences, societal attitudes, and systemic structures. Understanding these aspects is crucial for creating inclusive environments, fostering empathy, and addressing the diverse needs of individuals living with disabilities. Here are key considerations regarding the psychological and social dimensions of disability:

1. Psychological Impact:

- Identity and Self-esteem: Individuals with disabilities may grapple with issues of identity and self-esteem. Acceptance of one's disability and the ability to integrate it into one's self-concept are critical psychological processes.

- Coping Strategies: Coping with a disability involves developing effective strategies to manage stress, frustration, and potential mental health challenges. The ability to adapt to new circumstances and find resilience is vital.

- Emotional Well-being: The emotional well-being of individuals with disabilities can be influenced by societal perceptions, personal expectations, and the degree of social support available. Addressing emotional needs is integral to overall psychological health.

2. Social Dynamics:

- Stigmatization and Discrimination: Persons with disabilities often face societal stigmatization and discrimination, which can contribute to feelings of isolation and marginalization. These negative attitudes may impact various aspects of life, including education, employment, and social interactions.

- Social Isolation: Limited accessibility, physical barriers, and attitudinal barriers can result in social isolation. Exclusion from community activities and events can have profound effects on mental well-being.

- Relationships and Intimacy: Individuals with disabilities may navigate challenges in forming and maintaining relationships due to societal misconceptions and preconceived notions. Addressing these challenges involves fostering a more inclusive understanding of love and intimacy.

3. Access And Inclusion:

- Physical Access: The physical environment can pose significant challenges for individuals with disabilities. Lack of accessible infrastructure, transportation, and public spaces can limit mobility and independence.

- Inclusive Practices: Promoting inclusivity involves creating environments that accommodate diverse abilities. This includes accessible technology, adaptive equipment, and universal design principles to ensure equal opportunities for participation.

4. Employment And Education:

- Employment Discrimination: Individuals with disabilities may face discrimination in the workplace, affecting career opportunities and job satisfaction. Addressing these challenges requires inclusive employment practices and accommodations.

- Educational Barriers: Access to quality education may be hindered by a lack of accommodations and inclusive practices. Efforts are needed to ensure that educational environments cater to diverse learning needs.

5. Empowerment And Advocacy:

- Self-Advocacy: Empowering individuals with disabilities involves fostering self-advocacy skills. This includes advocating for personal needs, rights, and equal opportunities.

- Community Advocacy: Broader advocacy efforts aim to challenge societal norms, change perceptions, and promote policies that support inclusivity and equal access for individuals with disabilities.

6. Caregiver And Family Dynamics:

- Caregiver Stress: Families and caregivers of individuals with disabilities may experience stress and burnout. Providing support systems, education, and respite care is crucial for maintaining the well-being of both the individual and their support network.

- Family Inclusion: Fostering inclusive family dynamics involves recognizing the strengths and abilities of each family member, regardless of disability. Open communication and understanding contribute to a supportive family environment.

Understanding and addressing the psychological and social aspects of disability requires a comprehensive and empathetic approach. It involves challenging societal norms, advocating for inclusive policies, and promoting environments that recognize and celebrate the diverse abilities of every individual.

The Psychology Of Physical Handicap

The psychology of physical handicap involves examining the emotional, cognitive, and behavioral aspects of individuals living with physical disabilities. A physical handicap can impact various dimensions of a person's life, influencing their self-perception, relationships, and overall well-being. Understanding the psychological aspects of physical handicaps is crucial for providing effective support, fostering resilience, and promoting the inclusion of individuals with disabilities. Here are key considerations:

Identity And Self-Concept

Impact On Self-Identity: Individuals with physical handicaps may experience changes in their self-identity as they navigate the challenges posed by their condition. Acceptance of the disability and integration into one's self-concept are ongoing processes.

Self-Esteem: The perception of self-worth may be influenced by societal attitudes and personal beliefs about disability. Fostering positive self-esteem involves recognizing strengths, achievements, and capabilities.

Coping And Adaptation

Coping Strategies: Individuals with physical handicaps often develop unique coping strategies to manage the emotional and practical aspects of their condition. Adaptive coping mechanisms contribute to resilience and psychological well-being.

Adaptation To Change: Adjusting to a physical handicap involves adapting to changes in daily life, routines, and activities. The ability to navigate these changes positively is essential for psychological adjustment.

Social Dynamics

Stigmatization And Discrimination: Societal attitudes toward disability can contribute to stigmatization and discrimination. Negative perceptions may impact social interactions, relationships, and opportunities, influencing the individual's psychological well-being.

Social Support: The presence of a supportive social network is crucial for individuals with physical handicaps. Social support can buffer against the negative effects of societal attitudes and contribute to a positive psychological environment.

Emotional Well-Being

Mental Health Challenges: Individuals with physical handicaps may be more susceptible to mental health challenges, including depression and anxiety. Addressing emotional well-being involves providing access to mental health resources and support.

Resilience: Many individuals with physical handicaps demonstrate remarkable resilience in the face of adversity. Building resilience involves developing coping skills, a sense of purpose, and the ability to adapt to challenges.

Adaptive Technology And Independence

Role Of Technology: Adaptive technologies play a crucial role in enhancing independence and quality of life for individuals with physical handicaps. Access to assistive devices contributes to psychological well-being by facilitating greater autonomy.

Personal Empowerment: Providing individuals with the tools and resources to control their environment and engage in activities promotes a sense of personal empowerment. This empowerment positively influences psychological aspects such as self-efficacy and autonomy.

Employment And Educational Opportunities

Career Identity: Employment opportunities and career identity may be influenced by societal perceptions and workplace accommodations. Empowering individuals to pursue their professional aspirations involves addressing barriers to employment and education.

Inclusive Education: Inclusive educational practices contribute to positive psychological outcomes by providing individuals with physical handicaps equal access to educational opportunities and fostering a sense of belonging.

Understanding the psychology of physical handicap requires a holistic approach that recognizes the individual's strengths, resilience, and unique coping mechanisms. Fostering a supportive environment, challenging societal stereotypes, and promoting inclusivity contribute to the psychological well-being of individuals with physical handicaps. Additionally, recognizing and valuing the diverse abilities of each individual is fundamental to creating a more inclusive and empathetic society.

Chapter 6
Conclusion

Implementing a holistic and person-centered approach that involves collaboration between government agencies, non-profit organizations, communities, and individuals is a key to effectively addressing psychosocial problems among differently-abled persons.

In conclusion, differently-abled elderly individuals encounter a myriad of challenges that impact various facets of their lives. From physical limitations and social isolation to financial strain and a lack of inclusive policies, the difficulties faced by this demographic are complex and interconnected. Addressing these issues requires a comprehensive and compassionate approach that encompasses healthcare, social services, and community support.

The key to enhancing the well-being of differently-abled elderly persons lies in creating environments that are not only physically accessible but also socially and emotionally supportive. This involves implementing inclusive policies, promoting awareness about the diverse needs of this population, and fostering a culture of respect and understanding.

Moreover, acknowledging the psychological impact of disabilities in later life is crucial. Mental health support, tailored to the unique challenges faced by differently-abled elderly individuals, should be integrated into healthcare services. This includes addressing issues of self-identity, coping with change, and managing the emotional aspects of aging with a disability.

Caregiver support is another critical aspect, recognizing the often overlooked burden on family members and friends providing care. Providing resources, respite care, and educational programs for caregivers can contribute to a more sustainable and supportive caregiving environment.

Empowering differently-abled elderly individuals involves not only addressing their immediate needs but also promoting their active participation in society. This includes advocating for educational and recreational opportunities, fostering employment inclusivity, and cultivating a sense of community engagement.

In essence, solving the problems faced by differently-abled elderly individuals requires a collaborative effort from various sectors of society. Governments, communities, healthcare providers, and advocacy groups must work together to create an inclusive and supportive environment that allows every individual, regardless of ability, to age with dignity, independence, and a sense of belonging.

In conclusion, the psycho-social problems faced by differently-abled individuals are complex and multifaceted, encompassing both psychological and social dimensions. These challenges significantly impact the overall well-being and quality of life for individuals with disabilities. Addressing these issues requires a holistic and inclusive approach that considers the unique needs and experiences of each person. Here are key points to conclude on psycho-social problems among differently-abled persons:

1. **Identity And Self-Esteem:**
    - Differently-abled individuals often grapple with issues related to self-identity and self-esteem. Acceptance of their disability and integration into a society that may stigmatize or marginalize them can pose significant challenges.

2. **Social Isolation And Stigma:**
    - Social isolation and the stigma associated with disabilities contribute to a sense of exclusion. Limited social opportunities and negative perceptions from others can impact mental health and hinder social integration.

3. **Mental Health Struggles:**
   - Psychological challenges, including depression, anxiety, and stress, are common among differently-abled individuals. Coping with the demands of a society that may not fully understand or accommodate their needs can take a toll on mental well-being.

4. **Accessibility And Environmental Barriers:**
   - Physical and environmental barriers can restrict the mobility and independence of differently-abled individuals, leading to feelings of frustration and dependence. Inaccessible spaces contribute to a sense of exclusion.

5. **Educational And Employment Disparities:**
   - Limited access to education and employment opportunities can result in feelings of inadequacy and hinder personal development. Overcoming systemic barriers to inclusive education and employment is crucial for socio-economic empowerment.

6. **Relationship Challenges:**
   - Building and maintaining relationships can be challenging for differently-abled individuals, influenced by societal perceptions and personal insecurities. Addressing these challenges requires understanding and support from both individuals and communities.

7. **Discrimination And Prejudice:**
   - Discrimination and prejudice based on disability can lead to systemic inequalities and hinder social integration. Advocacy for anti-discrimination policies and public awareness campaigns are essential in combating these issues.

8. **Caregiver Stress:**
   - Family members and caregivers of differently-abled individuals may experience stress and burnout. Providing adequate support systems, respite care, and educational resources for caregivers is crucial for the well-being of both the individual and their support network.

9. **Advocacy And Inclusivity:**
   - Promoting advocacy efforts and inclusivity in various aspects of life, including education, employment, and social activities, is fundamental to addressing psycho-social problems. Creating a culture that values diversity and inclusion is essential for fostering a supportive environment.

10. **Empowerment And Independence:**
    - Empowering differently-abled individuals involves providing opportunities for skill development, promoting independence, and recognizing their contributions to society. This can positively impact self-esteem and overall mental well-being.

In conclusion, a concerted effort from society, policymakers, healthcare providers, and the community is necessary to address the psycho-social problems among differently-abled persons. Embracing diversity, fostering inclusivity, and advocating for systemic changes are vital steps toward creating a more supportive and understanding environment for individuals with disabilities.

Case Study 1: Kevin's Life Beyond The Bench

Kevin is a 55-year-old retired civil engineer who spends his days mentoring young professionals, volunteering at community events, and tinkering with woodworking projects in his garage. He's married with three grown children and is known for his sense of humor and love for his local baseball team.

Kevin has been living with Parkinson's disease for 12 years. When he first noticed the tremors in his hands and the stiffness in his movements, he brushed them off as stress-related. It wasn't until he had difficulty holding his tools steady during a project that he sought medical advice and received the diagnosis.

Though the news was devastating at first, Kevin decided he wouldn't let Parkinson's define his life. He continued working for another five years, adapting his tasks to focus on project planning rather than hands-on engineering. After retiring, Kevin found new ways to stay active and engaged.

One of Kevin's biggest frustrations is the way people perceive him. "When I'm out in public and my hand trembles, people sometimes assume I'm nervous or weak," he explains. "I wish they could see past that." He also faces physical barriers, such as restaurants with narrow aisles that make it hard to maneuver comfortably.

Kevin finds purpose in sharing his story to raise awareness about Parkinson's. He speaks at community events and supports others newly diagnosed with the condition. His woodworking projects, though slower now, have become a therapeutic outlet and a way to create gifts for friends and family.

One memorable moment for Kevin was when his grandson asked him to help build a treehouse. Although it took longer than expected and required adjustments for Kevin's physical limitations, the finished product was a labor of love that brought the family closer together.

"Life isn't perfect, but it's still beautiful," Kevin says. "I focus on what I can do rather than what I can't, and I hope that inspires others to do the same."

Case Study 2: Ethan's Journey Of Independence And Advocacy

Ethan is a 48-year-old father of two teenage daughters. A software developer by profession, he loves hiking, gardening, and cooking with his family. Ethan is also an avid reader and enjoys participating in local book clubs. However, Ethan has been living with a disability for nearly 25 years after a car accident in 1999 left him with quadriplegia.

Despite the severity of his injury, Ethan's life is a testament to resilience and adaptability. He uses a motorized wheelchair and advanced assistive technologies to maintain his independence. His journey has been supported by organizations like **Pathfinder Care** in Tasmania, which provided him with physical and occupational therapy, adaptive equipment, and counseling to rebuild his life after the accident.

Initially, Ethan faced significant physical and emotional challenges. Simple tasks like eating or typing required extensive training and support. **Pathfinder Care** introduced him to assistive devices like a mouth-operated joystick for his wheelchair and voice-recognition software for his computer. With their guidance, Ethan was able to return to his job as a software developer within three years of his accident.

Ethan's life is not defined by his disability. "I'm just a regular guy who's had to adapt a little more than most," he says. He works full-time, manages his household finances, and attends all his daughters' school events. With the help of **Pathfinder Care**, he also pursued hobbies he thought he'd lost forever, like gardening. They helped design an accessible garden space with raised beds and automatic watering systems, allowing Ethan to continue his passion.

Ethan has also faced societal barriers. Public events, such as concerts or fairs, often lack adequate accessibility, making it challenging for him to attend with his family. In one instance, a staff member at a local theater assumed Ethan would need a caregiver and attempted to separate him from his family during seating arrangements. "It's not the wheelchair that limits me," Ethan explains, "it's the assumptions people make about what I can or cannot do."

Ethan has become an advocate for disability rights, inspired by **Pathfinder Care's** philosophy of empowerment. He works with the organization to mentor newly injured individuals, teaching them how to navigate life with confidence and dignity. **"Pathfinder Care** didn't just give me tools—they gave me hope," Ethan says.

Case Study 3: Susan's Journey: A Mother And Advocate

Susan is a 45-year-old single mother of two teenagers. She has been living with multiple sclerosis (MS) for 15 years, a condition that has progressively limited her mobility and stamina. Despite her challenges, Susan has always been determined to live an active life. Before her diagnosis, Susan worked as a graphic designer and loved hiking and kayaking.

After her diagnosis, Susan faced numerous barriers. Her office was not wheelchair-accessible, forcing her to work remotely, which ultimately led to her feeling isolated. Public transportation was another challenge, often lacking accommodations for wheelchairs. However, Susan's greatest hurdle was societal perceptions—people often assumed she couldn't be an effective mother due to her condition.

With the help of **Pathfinder Care**, Susan found tailored support to regain her independence. **Pathfinder's Care** team assisted her with home modifications, including accessible kitchens and ramps. They also introduced her to their adaptive kayaking program, rekindling her love for the sport. Additionally, **Pathfinder's Care** counseling sessions helped Susan address her mental health and empowered her to become an advocate for accessible public spaces.

Today, Susan is a spokesperson for disability rights, working with **Pathfinder Care** to raise awareness about the importance of inclusive communities. She says, "**Pathfinder Care** gave me the tools and confidence to reclaim my life. I'm a better mother and a stronger advocate because of their support."

Case Study 4: Maria's Path To Independence: A Young Entrepreneur

Maria, 28, was born with cerebral palsy and has used a wheelchair since childhood. Growing up in a small Tasmanian town, Maria faced significant barriers to education and employment. Despite his sharp mind and love for technology, many schools lacked proper resources to support his learning needs. Determined to break stereotypes, Maria completed his degree in computer science through an online university program. However, finding a job proved to be another challenge. Employers often overlooked him, assuming his disability would hinder his productivity.

Pathfinder Care became a turning point in Maria's life. They offered job readiness programs, connecting him with inclusive employers. Through their mentorship, Maria launched his own IT consultancy, specializing in creating accessible websites and software.

Pathfinder's Care also provided solutions to Psycho social Problems Among Differently-Abled Elderly Persons, financial aid for assistive technology, including voice-controlled devices that enhanced Maria's efficiency.

Maria now runs a successful business and mentors young individuals with disabilities through **Pathfinder's Care** youth programs. "**Pathfinder Care** didn't just help me; they believed in me," Maria shares. "They opened doors I didn't know existed."

Case Study 5: Antonio's Fight for Accessibility in Sports

Antonio, 17, is a high school student with spina bifida who has always dreamed of becoming a professional swimmer. While his school encouraged athletic participation, it lacked the facilities and coaching expertise to support adaptive sports. Antonio often found himself sidelined during physical education classes and competitive events.

When Antonio's family connected with **Pathfinder Care**, his world changed. **Pathfinder Care** partnered with local organizations to develop an adaptive swimming program, providing him access to specialized coaches and equipment. They also advocated for Antonio's inclusion in school sports, working with educators to create more inclusive policies.

Antonio's hard work paid off—he recently won a silver medal in a national para-swimming competition. He now aims to qualify for the Paralympic Games. "**Pathfinder Care** believed in my potential when others didn't. They showed me that my dreams are valid," Antonio says.

The Role of Pathfinder Care

Located in Tasmania, **Pathfinder Care** plays a pivotal role in transforming the lives of individuals with disabilities. Their comprehensive approach includes:

- **Rehabilitation Services**: Offering tailored physical and mental health support.
- **Skill Development**: Providing job readiness, financial literacy, and life skills training.
- **Recreational Opportunities**: Organizing adaptive sports and community programs.
- **Advocacy And Awareness**: Collaborating with local governments and organizations to promote inclusivity and accessibility.

Through personalized care and community integration, **Pathfinder Care** ensures that individuals with disabilities can lead fulfilling, independent lives, breaking barriers and achieving their goals.

References:

1. https://www.nhfdc.nic.in/upload/nhfdc/Persons_Disabilities_31 mar21.pdf
2. https://www.cdc.gov/ncbddd/disabilityandhealth/infographic-disability-impacts-all.html
3. Australian Bureau of Statistics (25 September 2020), Psychosocial disability, ABS Website, accessed 6 February 2024.
4. Australian Bureau of Statistics. (2020, September 25). *Psychosocial disability*. ABS. https://www.abs.gov.au/articles/psychosocial-disability.
5. Australian Bureau of Statistics. "Psychosocial disability." *ABS*, 25 September 2020, https://www.abs.gov.au/articles/psychosocial-disability.
6. Australian Bureau of Statistics. *Psychosocial disability* [Internet]. Canberra: ABS; 2020 September 25. Available from: https://www.abs.gov.au/articles/psychosocial-disability.
7. Australian Bureau of Statistics 2020, *Psychosocial disability*, ABS, https://www.abs.gov.au/articles/psychosocial-disability
8. https://www.gov.uk/government/statistics/family-resources-survey-financial-year-2021-to-2022

www.ingramcontent.com/pod-product-compliance
Lightning Source LLC
LaVergne TN
LVHW061601070526
838199LV00077B/7133